contents

Don't Call me, you have this Book to help you

Masi xx

Enjoy .

NZ, Canada, US and UK readers
Please note that Australian cup and spoon
measurements are metric. A quick conversion
guide appears on page 63.

baking information

oven types and rack position

If you have a fan-forced oven, check the operating instructions; as a rule, reduce the temperature by 10°C to 20°C when using the fan during baking, and be aware that baking times might be less than specified.

When baking, position the oven racks and cake pan(s) so that the top of the baked item is roughly in the centre of the oven. Several items can be baked at the same time, but the pans shouldn't touch each other, or the oven wall or door, to allow even circulation of heat. To ensure even browning, swap the positions of cake pans on different racks about halfway through baking time.

how to prepare cake pans

To grease a cake pan, use either a light, even coating of cooking-oil spray, or brush melted butter or margarine evenly over the base and side(s). Cakes with a high sugar content have a tendency to stick so we recommend lining the base and/or side(s) of their pans with baking paper.

to test if a cake is cooked

All cake-baking times are approximate. Check your cake at the suggested cooking time; it should be browned and starting to shrink from the side(s) of the pan, and the top should feel firm. In all cakes, except a sponge, insert a thin metal skewer into the deepest part of the cake from top to base. Gently remove the skewer; it shouldn't have any uncooked mixture clinging to it.

cooling cakes

We have suggested standing cakes for various times then turning onto wire racks to cool. The best way to do this is to gently shake the cake pan to loosen the cake. Turn the cake, upside down, onto wire rack, then turn the cake top-side up immediately using a second rack (unless directed otherwise).

tips and tricks

- Always have the ingredients at room temperature, particularly butter. Melted or extremely soft butter will alter the texture of the baked item.
- When measuring liquids, always stand the marked measuring jug on a flat surface and check at eye level for accuracy.
- Spoon and cup measurements should be levelled off with a knife or spatula.

Grease cake pan with pastry brush and melted butter

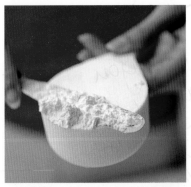

Level top of measuring cup with a spatula

chocolate techniques

how to melt chocolate

Melting chocolate is not difficult if you follow a few rules. Everything you use (saucepan, stirring spoon, even your hands) must be absolutely dry; any droplets of water in the chocolate will cause it to seize, that is, clump and turn grey. Another thing to avoid when melting chocolate is excessive use of direct heat. No matter what method you choose to melt chocolate, patience is paramount.

microwave-oven method

Place coarsely chopped chocolate in a small microwave-safe bowl; heat on MEDIUM power (55%) for 15 to 20 second intervals, pausing to stir gently between times. When the chocolate is almost melted, remove from the microwave oven and allow it to sit for a minute to complete the melting process.

cook top method

Place a little water in a small saucepan – make sure the water does not touch the bottom of your choice of small heatproof bowl (a glass or china bowl is best) when it is fitted inside the pan. Cover pan and bring the water to a boil. Remove lid from pan and reduce heat to a slow simmer. Place coarsely chopped chocolate in a small heatproof bowl; sit bowl, uncovered, over the simmering water until chocolate is melted, stirring occasionally. After chocolate has melted, carefully remove the bowl from the water and wipe underside of bowl dry.

how to grate chocolate

Be sure the piece of chocolate you intend to grate is cool and firm. Use a hand grater, and clean the grater often so the chocolate doesn't clog the surface of the blade. You can also "grate" chocolate in a blender – this is especially good if you're grating a lot of chocolate – but be sure to chop the chocolate coarsely first.

how to make chocolate curls

For small curls, scrape a sharp vegetable peeler along the side of a long piece of room-temperature eating-quality chocolate. For larger curls, spread melted chocolate evenly onto a clean, flat oven tray, cutting board or piece of marble; stand until just set, but not hard. Scrape a large flat knife across chocolate, pulling curls off with every movement. If curls resemble shavings, the chocolate is too cold. Curls can be stored in an airtight container at room temperature or in the refrigerator if the weather is hot.

Stir melting chocolate gently between bursts of microwave power

Scrape a large, flat knife across chocolate to make large curls

chocolate sponge

3 eggs
½ cup (110g) caster sugar
¼ cup (35g) cornflour
¼ cup (35g) plain flour
¼ cup (35g) self-raising flour
2 tablespoons cocoa powder
300ml thickened cream, whipped
coffee icing
3 teaspoons instant coffee powder
2 tablespoons milk
1½ cups (240g) icing sugar mixture
1 teaspoon soft butter

Preheat oven to moderate. Grease deep 22cm-round
cake pan; line base with baking paper.
Beat eggs in small bowl with electric mixer about 8 minutes
or until thick and creamy. Gradually add sugar, beating
until dissolved between each addition. Transfer mixture
to large bowl; gently fold in triple-sifted dry ingredients.
Spread mixture into prepared pan.
Bake in moderate oven about 25 minutes. Turn sponge
immediately onto wire rack to cool.
Split sponge in half; join with cream. Spread top with
coffee icing; leave to set before cutting.
Coffee icing Combine coffee and milk in small bowl;
stir until dissolved. Sift icing sugar into small bowl; stir in
butter and enough of the coffee mixture to give a firm paste.
Stir over hot water until icing is spreadable; do not over-heat.
Use immediately.

serves 8 to 10
tips This cake is best made on the day of serving.
The unfilled and un-iced cake is suitable to freeze.
The coffee icing is suitable to microwave.

family chocolate cake

2 cups (500ml) water
3 cups (660g)
   caster sugar
250g butter, chopped
⅓ cup (35g)
   cocoa powder
1 teaspoon bicarbonate
   of soda
3 cups (450g)
   self-raising flour
4 eggs, beaten lightly
fudge frosting
90g butter
⅓ cup (80ml) water
½ cup (110g)
   caster sugar
1½ cups (240g) icing
   sugar mixture
⅓ cup (35g)
   cocoa powder

Preheat oven to moderate. Grease deep
26.5cm x 33cm (14 cup/3.5 litre) baking dish;
line base with baking paper.

Combine the water, sugar, butter and combined
sifted cocoa powder and soda in medium saucepan;
stir over heat, without boiling, until sugar dissolves.
Bring to a boil then reduce heat; simmer, uncovered,
5 minutes. Transfer mixture to large bowl; cool to
room temperature.

Add flour and egg to bowl; beat with electric
mixer until mixture is smooth and changed to
a paler colour. Pour mixture into prepared dish.

Bake cake in moderate oven about 50 minutes.
Stand cake in baking dish 10 minutes, before
turning onto wire rack; turn cake top-side up to
cool. Spread cold cake with fudge frosting.

Fudge frosting Combine butter, the water and
caster sugar in small saucepan; stir over heat,
without boiling, until sugar dissolves. Sift icing sugar
and cocoa powder into small bowl then gradually
stir in hot butter mixture. Cover; refrigerate about
20 minutes or until frosting thickens. Beat with
wooden spoon until spreadable.

serves 20
tips Choose a perfectly level-bottomed baking
dish; one made from cast aluminium is the best
choice, but almost any type will work.
If the cake appears to be cooking too quickly in
the corners of the pan, reduce oven temperature
to moderately slow; this will increase cooking time
by up to 15 minutes.

devil's food cake

180g butter, chopped
1¾ cups (385g) caster sugar
3 eggs
1½ cups (225g) self-raising flour
½ cup (75g) plain flour
½ teaspoon bicarbonate of soda
⅔ cup (70g) cocoa powder
3 teaspoons instant coffee powder
½ teaspoon red food colouring
½ cup (125ml) water
½ cup (125ml) milk
300ml thickened cream, whipped
rich chocolate frosting
60g dark eating chocolate, chopped
60g butter, chopped

Preheat oven to moderate. Grease two deep 20cm-round cake pans; line bases with baking paper, then grease paper.
Beat butter and sugar in small bowl with electric mixer until light and fluffy; add eggs, one at a time, beating well after each addition.
Transfer mixture to large bowl; fold in sifted flours, soda and cocoa powder with combined coffee, colouring, water and milk, in two batches. Pour mixture into prepared pans.
Bake in moderate oven about 45 minutes. Turn cakes onto wire racks to cool.
Join cold cakes with whipped cream; top with rich chocolate frosting.
Rich chocolate frosting Combine chocolate and butter in heatproof bowl over pan of simmering water; stir until smooth. Remove from heat. Cool at room temperature until spreadable; stir occasionally while cooling.

serves 8 to 10
tips The un-iced cake can be made two days ahead; store in an airtight container. The un-iced cake is suitable to freeze. The rich chocolate frosting is suitable to microwave.

chocolate peppermint cake

125g butter, chopped

2 teaspoons instant
  coffee powder

¾ cup (180ml) water

100g dark eating chocolate,
  chopped coarsely

1 cup (220g)
  caster sugar

1 egg, beaten lightly

¾ cup (110g)
  self-raising flour

½ cup (75g) plain flour

2 tablespoons
  cocoa powder

peppermint cream

125g butter, chopped

3 cups (480g) icing
  sugar mixture

2 tablespoons milk

½ teaspoon
  peppermint essence

green food colouring

chocolate ganache

300g dark eating chocolate,
  chopped coarsely

1 cup (250ml) cream

Preheat oven to slow. Grease two
8cm x 26cm bar cake pans; line bases
and sides with baking paper.

Stir butter, coffee, the water, chocolate and
sugar in medium saucepan over heat until
smooth. Transfer mixture to medium bowl.
Whisk in egg with sifted flours and cocoa powder.
Pour mixture equally between prepared pans.

Bake in slow oven about 45 minutes. Stand
cakes in pans 5 minutes, before turning top-side
up onto wire rack to cool.

Using serrated knife, split cooled cakes in half.
Place bottom layers on wire rack over tray.
Spread each with about a quarter of the
peppermint cream; top with cake tops.

Place remaining peppermint cream in piping bag
fitted with 2cm fluted tube. Pipe remaining cream
along centre of each cake top; refrigerate 1 hour.

Using metal spatula and working quickly, pour
chocolate ganache over cakes, smoothing sides.
Stand at room temperature until ganache sets.

Peppermint cream Beat butter in small bowl
with electric mixer until as pale as possible.
Gradually beat in sifted icing sugar, milk,
essence and enough of the colouring to
tint to the desired shade of green.

Chocolate ganache Combine chocolate
and cream in small saucepan; stir over
low heat until smooth.

serves 20

tips The un-iced cake is suitable to freeze.
The chocolate ganache is suitable to microwave.

mocha syrup cake

3 teaspoons instant coffee powder
1 tablespoon hot water
3 eggs
¾ cup (165g) caster sugar
1 cup (150g) self-raising flour
1 tablespoon cocoa powder
150g butter, melted
coffee syrup
¾ cup (165g) caster sugar
¾ cup (180ml) water
3 teaspoons instant coffee powder

Preheat oven to moderate. Grease 21cm baba
cake pan.
Combine coffee and the water; stir until dissolved.
Beat eggs in small bowl with electric mixer about
8 minutes or until thick and creamy. Gradually add sugar;
beat until dissolved between each addition.
Transfer to large bowl, fold in sifted flour and cocoa powder,
then butter and coffee mixture. Pour mixture into prepared pan.
Bake in moderate oven about 40 minutes. Stand cake
in pan 5 minutes, before turning onto baking-paper-covered
wire rack, stand wire rack over a tray.
Reserve ¼ cup of the hot coffee syrup. Pour remaining
syrup over hot cake. Serve drizzled with reserved syrup.
Coffee syrup Combine ingredients in small saucepan;
stir over heat, without boiling, until sugar is dissolved. Bring
to a boil, remove from heat; transfer syrup to heatproof jug.

serves 8
tip This cake can be made a day ahead; store in
an airtight container.

chocolate fruit cake

125g butter, chopped
¾ cup (150g) firmly packed brown sugar
50g dark eating chocolate, chopped coarsely
½ cup (125ml) water
¼ cup (60ml) dark rum
¼ cup (30g) coarsely chopped walnuts
½ cup (75g) dried currants
1 cup (160g) sultanas
1 cup (170g) coarsely chopped raisins
¼ cup (40g) mixed peel
¾ cup (110g) plain flour
2 tablespoons cocoa powder
2 tablespoons self-raising flour
½ teaspoon mixed spice
2 eggs, beaten lightly
80g dark eating chocolate, melted, extra
¼ cup (60g) sour cream

Preheat oven to slow. Grease 20cm ring pan;
line base with baking paper.
Combine butter, sugar, chocolate and the water in
medium saucepan; stir over heat until sugar dissolves.
Remove from heat; stir in rum, nuts and fruit.
Add sifted dry ingredients and egg; stir until combined.
Spoon mixture into prepared pan.
Bake in slow oven about 1 hour. Cool cake in pan.
Just before serving, combine cooled extra chocolate
and sour cream in small bowl; stir until smooth. Turn cake
onto serving plate, top-side up; spread chocolate mixture
over top of cake.

serves 12
tip If preferred, this cake can be baked in a 14cm x 21cm
loaf pan; bake in a slow oven about 1½ hours.

chocolate buttermilk cake

180g butter, chopped
1 teaspoon vanilla essence
1½ cups (330g) caster sugar
4 eggs, separated
¾ cup (110g) self-raising flour
⅓ cup (35g) cocoa powder
¾ cup (180ml) buttermilk
chocolate filling
400g dark eating chocolate, melted
250g butter, melted
½ cup (80g) icing sugar mixture

Preheat oven to moderate. Grease deep 20cm-round cake pan; line base with baking paper.

Beat butter, essence and sugar in small bowl with electric mixer until light and fluffy; beat in egg yolks, one at a time, until just combined. Transfer mixture to large bowl; stir in sifted dry ingredients and buttermilk.

Beat egg whites in clean small bowl with electric mixer until soft peaks form; fold into cake mixture in two batches. Pour cake mixture into prepared pan.

Bake in moderate oven about 1 hour. Cool cake in pan.

Split cake into three layers. Reserve about 1 cup of the chocolate filling. Place one cake layer onto serving plate, spread thinly with some of the remaining chocolate filling; repeat layering with remaining cake layers and filling. Spread reserved filling all over cake. Refrigerate 3 hours before serving.

Chocolate filling Combine chocolate and butter in medium bowl; stir in sifted icing sugar. Cool filling to room temperature; beat with wooden spoon until thick and spreadable.

serves 8 to 10
tips This cake can be made a day ahead and kept, covered, in the refrigerator.
The butter and chocolate are suitable to microwave.

black forest cake

250g butter, chopped
1 tablespoon instant coffee powder
1½ cups (375ml) hot water
200g dark eating chocolate, chopped
2 cups (440g) caster sugar
1½ cups (225g) self-raising flour
1 cup (150g) plain flour
¼ cup (25g) cocoa powder
2 eggs
2 teaspoons vanilla essence
600ml thickened cream
¼ cup (60ml) kirsch
2 x 425g cans cherries, drained, halved

Preheat oven to slow. Grease deep 22cm-round cake pan; line base and side with baking paper.
Melt butter in medium saucepan; stir in combined coffee and hot water, then chocolate and sugar. Stir over low heat, without boiling, until smooth. Transfer mixture to large bowl, cool to warm.
Beat mixture on low speed with electric mixer; gradually beat in sifted dry ingredients in three batches. Beat in eggs, one at a time, then essence. Pour mixture into prepared pan.
Bake in slow oven about 1¾ hours. Stand cake in pan 5 minutes, before turning onto wire rack to cool.
Beat cream until firm peaks form. Trim top of cake to make it flat. Split cake into three even layers. Place one layer on serving plate, brush with one third of the kirsch; top with one third of the cream and half of the cherries. Repeat layering once more, then top with cake-top. Brush top of cake with remaining kirsch; spread with remaining cream. Decorate with fresh cherries and chocolate curls, if desired.

serves 10 to 12

white chocolate mud cake

*The white chocolate mud cake has rapidly ascended the ladder
to the top of the special-occasion favourite-cake list.*

250g butter, chopped
150g white cooking
  chocolate, chopped
2 cups (440g)
  caster sugar
1 cup (250ml) milk
1½ cups (225g)
  plain flour
½ cup (75g)
  self-raising flour
1 teaspoon
  vanilla essence
2 eggs, beaten lightly
white chocolate
  ganache
½ cup (125ml) cream
300g white cooking
  chocolate, chopped

Preheat oven to moderately slow. Grease
deep 20cm-round cake pan; line base and side
with baking paper.

Combine butter, chocolate, sugar and milk in
medium saucepan; using wooden spoon, stir over
low heat, without boiling, until smooth. Transfer
mixture to large bowl; cool 15 minutes.

Whisk in flours then essence and egg; pour mixture
into prepared pan.

Bake in moderately slow oven 1 hour. Cover pan
loosely with foil; bake about 1 hour. Discard foil,
stand cake in pan 10 minutes then turn onto wire rack;
turn top-side up to cool.

Place cake on serving plate, spread all over with
white chocolate ganache.

White chocolate ganache Bring cream to a boil
in small saucepan; pour over chocolate in small bowl,
stir with wooden spoon until chocolate melts. Cover
bowl; refrigerate, stirring occasionally, about 30 minutes
or until ganache is of a spreadable consistency.

serves 12

tips It can be difficult to determine if this cake is
cooked. The best guide is to follow the baking times
provided, plus the crust on the finished cake should
feel thick and sugary.
The un-iced cake will keep for up to one week in an
airtight container at room temperature. The iced cake
will keep for up to one week in an airtight container
in the refrigerator.

sacher torte

150g dark eating
  chocolate, chopped
1 tablespoon warm water
150g butter, chopped
½ cup (110g) caster sugar
3 eggs, separated
1 cup (150g) plain flour
2 tablespoons caster
  sugar, extra
²/₃ cup (220g) apricot jam
chocolate icing
125g dark eating
  chocolate, chopped
125g butter

Preheat oven to moderate. Grease
deep 22cm-round cake pan; line base
with baking paper.

Melt chocolate in heatproof bowl over hot water,
stir in the water; cool to room temperature.

Beat butter and sugar in small bowl with
electric mixer until pale in colour. Beat in
egg yolks, one at a time; beat until combined.
Transfer mixture to large bowl; stir in chocolate
mixture, then sifted flour.

Beat egg whites in small bowl until soft peaks
form, gradually add extra sugar, beat until
dissolved between each addition; fold lightly
into chocolate mixture. Spread mixture into
prepared pan.

Bake in moderate oven about 30 minutes.
Stand cake in pan 5 minutes, before turning
onto wire rack to cool; leave cake upside down.

Split cold cake in half, place one half onto serving
plate. Heat and strain jam, brush over half of the
cake. Top with remaining half of cake, brush cake
all over with remaining jam. Stand about 1 hour
at room temperature to allow jam to set.

Spread top and side of cake with chocolate icing;
set at room temperature.

Chocolate icing Melt chocolate and butter in
medium bowl over hot water, stir until smooth.
Cool to room temperature until spreadable, stir
occasionally; this can take up to 2 hours.

serves 10 to 12
tip This icing is also suitable for piping.

chocolate ganache and raspberry cake

⅓ cup (35g) cocoa powder
⅓ cup (80ml) hot water
150g dark eating chocolate, chopped
150g butter, chopped
1⅓ cups (300g) firmly packed brown sugar
1 cup (125g) almond meal
4 eggs, separated
240g fresh raspberries
chocolate ganache
200g dark eating chocolate, chopped
⅔ cup (160ml) thickened cream

Preheat oven to moderately slow. Grease deep 22cm-round cake pan; line base and side with baking paper.

Blend cocoa powder with the hot water in small bowl until smooth.

Combine chocolate and butter in medium heatproof bowl over saucepan of simmering water; stir until melted. Remove from heat; stir in cocoa mixture, sugar, almond meal and egg yolks.

Beat egg whites in clean small bowl with an electric mixer until soft peaks form; fold into chocolate mixture in two batches. Pour mixture into prepared pan.

Bake in moderately slow oven about 1¼ hours. Stand cake in pan 15 minutes, before turning onto wire rack to cool.

Arrange berries on cake; pour chocolate ganache over cake to partially cover the berries. Stand at room temperature until set.

Chocolate ganache Combine chocolate and cream in small saucepan; stir over low heat until smooth.

serves 12

tip This cake can be made up to three days ahead; store in an airtight container. Top with berries and chocolate ganache on the day of serving.

rich truffle mud cake

This very rich cake is perfect for the grand finale to a dinner party, and should be made a day ahead and served cold. The cake is almost like a huge truffle in texture; note that no flour is used.

6 eggs
½ cup (110g) firmly packed brown sugar
400g dark eating chocolate, melted
1 cup (250ml) thick cream
⅓ cup (80ml) Cointreau

Preheat oven to moderate. Grease deep 22cm-round cake pan; line base and side with baking paper.
Beat eggs and sugar in large bowl with electric mixer about 5 minutes or until thick and creamy. With motor operating, gradually beat in barely warm chocolate; beat until combined.
Using metal spoon, gently fold in combined cream and liqueur. Pour mixture into prepared pan. Place pan in baking dish; pour enough boiling water into dish to come halfway up side of pan.
Bake cake in moderate oven 30 minutes. Cover loosely with foil; bake about 30 minutes. Discard foil; cool cake in pan.
Turn cake onto serving plate, cover; refrigerate overnight. Serve dusted with a little sifted cocoa powder, if desired.

serves 12 to 14
tips Any liqueur can be substituted for the citrus-flavoured Cointreau, if you prefer; try rum or Frangelico.
This cake is delicious served with fresh raspberries and fresh raspberry coulis.
Rich truffle mud cake will keep for up to four days in an airtight container in the refrigerator.

tiramisu cake

125g butter
2 teaspoons instant
  coffee powder
¾ cup (180ml) hot water
100g dark eating chocolate,
  chopped
1 cup (220g) caster sugar
¾ cup (110g)
  self-raising flour
½ cup (75g) plain flour
2 tablespoons
  cocoa powder
1 egg
1 teaspoon vanilla essence
1½ cups (375ml) water,
  extra
½ cup (110g) caster sugar,
  extra
¼ cup (10g) instant coffee
  powder, extra
2 tablespoons marsala
1 cup (250g) mascarpone
  cheese
300ml thick cream
120g raspberries
1 tablespoon cocoa
  powder, extra

Preheat oven to slow. Grease 23cm-square cake pan; line base with baking paper.

Combine butter, coffee powder, the hot water, chocolate and sugar in medium saucepan; stir over low heat until chocolate is melted. Place chocolate mixture in large bowl; cool 5 minutes.

Whisk in sifted flours and cocoa powder, in two batches; whisk in egg and essence. Pour mixture into prepared pan.

Bake in slow oven about 40 minutes. Stand cake in pan 5 minutes, before turning onto wire rack to cool.

Meanwhile, combine the extra water, extra sugar and extra coffee in medium saucepan; stir over heat, without boiling, until sugar is dissolved. Bring to a boil; boil, uncovered, without stirring, 5 minutes. Remove from heat, stir in marsala; cool. Reserve 1/3 cup of the coffee syrup.

Split cake in half horizontally. Place halves, crust-side up, on tray; brush with remaining coffee syrup. Cover; refrigerate 3 hours or overnight.

Cut each cake half into eight equal pieces. Combine mascarpone, cream and reserved coffee syrup in medium bowl; whisk gently until mixture thickens slightly.

Assemble tiramisu among eight serving dishes; place a piece of cake on each dish, top using half of the mascarpone mixture. Repeat, using remaining cake and mascarpone mixture. Top with raspberries; dust with extra sifted cocoa powder.

serves 8

double-decker mud cake

250g butter, chopped
150g white cooking chocolate, chopped
2 cups (440g) caster sugar
1 cup (250ml) milk
1½ cups (225g) plain flour
½ cup (75g) self-raising flour
1 teaspoon vanilla essence
2 eggs, beaten lightly
2 tablespoons cocoa powder
600g milk cooking chocolate, chopped coarsely
1 cup (250ml) cream

Preheat oven to slow. Grease two deep 20cm-round
cake pans; line bases and sides with baking paper.
Combine butter, white chocolate, sugar and milk in medium
saucepan; stir over heat, without boiling, until smooth.
Transfer mixture to large bowl; cool 15 minutes.
Whisk sifted flours into white chocolate mixture then
whisk in essence and egg; pour half of the mixture into
one of the prepared pans. Whisk sifted cocoa powder into
remaining mixture; pour into other prepared pan.
Bake cakes in slow oven about 50 minutes. Stand
cakes in pans 5 minutes; turn cakes, top-side up,
onto wire rack to cool.
Combine milk chocolate and cream in medium saucepan;
stir over low heat until smooth. Transfer to medium bowl.
Cover; refrigerate, stirring occasionally, until chocolate
mixture is of a spreadable consistency. Reserve 1 cup
of the chocolate mixture for spreading over cake.
Split each cooled cake in half. Place one layer of cake
on serving plate; spread with ½ cup of the remaining milk
chocolate mixture. Repeat layering, alternating colours. Cover
top and sides of cake with reserved chocolate mixture.

serves 10

rich chocolate meringue and mousse cake

8 egg whites
2 cups (220g)
  caster sugar
1/3 cup (35g)
  cocoa powder
2 tablespoons flaked
  almonds, toasted
75g red currants
120g raspberries
mousse filling
1/2 cup (55g)
  hazelnut meal
2 teaspoons gelatine
1 tablespoon water
300g dark eating
  chocolate, melted
8 egg yolks
1 tablespoon Tia Maria
600ml thickened cream

Preheat oven to very slow. Cover four oven trays with baking paper, mark 23cm-circles on paper.
Beat 4 of the egg whites in large bowl with electric mixer until soft peaks form. Gradually add 1 cup of the sugar, beat until dissolved between additions. Fold in 2 tablespoons of the sifted cocoa powder.
Divide mixture between two of the prepared trays, spread evenly within the marked circles.
Bake in very slow oven about 1 hour or until dry; cool in oven with door ajar. Repeat method using remaining egg white, sugar and cocoa; bake as before.
Place a meringue circle on serving plate, spread with a third of the mousse filling; repeat layers with remaining meringue circles and mousse filling, ending with a meringue layer. Refrigerate several hours or overnight.
Just before serving, decorate cake with almonds, currants and berries.
Mousse filling Preheat oven to moderate. Spread hazelnut meal on oven tray, toast in moderate oven about 5 minutes; cool. Sprinkle gelatine over the water in small heatproof jug, stand in small pan of simmering water, stir until gelatine is dissolved; cool to room temperature. Combine nuts, gelatine, chocolate, egg yolks and Tia Maria in large bowl. Beat cream, in small bowl, until soft peaks form; fold into chocolate mixture in two batches. Cover, refrigerate until firm.

serves 10
tip This cake is best assembled a day before serving; store, covered, in the refrigerator.

almond meringue cake

The combined textures of the soft cake, crisp meringue, crunchy nuts, rich berries and billows of whipped cream make this dessert cake manna from heaven. It's best made on the day of serving.

125g butter, chopped
½ cup (110g) caster sugar
3 eggs, separated
1 cup (150g) self-raising flour
⅓ cup (35g) cocoa powder
½ cup (125ml) buttermilk

½ cup (120g) sour cream
⅔ cup (150g) caster sugar, extra
2 tablespoons flaked almonds
⅔ cup (160ml) thickened cream
1 tablespoon icing sugar mixture
150g raspberries

Preheat oven to moderate. Grease two deep 22cm-round cake pans; line bases with baking paper.

Beat butter, sugar and egg yolks in medium bowl with electric mixer until light and fluffy. Using wooden spoon, stir in combined sifted flour and cocoa powder, then combined buttermilk and sour cream. Divide mixture evenly between prepared pans.

Beat egg whites in small bowl with electric mixer until soft peaks form; gradually add extra sugar, 1 tablespoon at a time, beating until sugar dissolves between additions. Divide meringue mixture evenly over cake mixture in pans; using metal spatula, spread meringue so cake mixture is completely covered. Sprinkle nuts over the meringue on one of the cakes.

Bake cakes in moderate oven 10 minutes. Cover pans loosely with foil; bake about 20 minutes. Discard foil; stand cakes in pans 5 minutes, before turning onto wire racks. Quickly and carefully turn cakes top-side up to cool.

Beat cream and icing sugar in small bowl with electric mixer until firm peaks form. Place cake without almonds on serving plate; spread cream over top, sprinkle evenly with raspberries, top with remaining cake.

serves 12

tips These cakes are quite fragile so, after turning cakes out of the pans, it's best to use two wire racks to turn them top-side up. If you have two 22cm springform tins, use them for baking these cakes so there is no need to turn the cakes.

This cake will keep for one day in an airtight container in the refrigerator.

flourless chocolate dessert cake

This crusty-topped cake will sink slightly as it cools.

100g dark eating chocolate, chopped
100g butter, chopped
2 tablespoons marsala
½ cup (110g) caster sugar
²/₃ cup (80g) almond meal
1 tablespoon instant coffee powder
1 tablespoon hot water
3 eggs, separated
icing sugar mixture
strawberry coulis
250g strawberries
¼ cup (40g) icing sugar mixture

Preheat oven to moderate. Grease deep 20cm-round cake pan; line base and side with baking paper.
Combine chocolate and butter in small saucepan; stir over low heat until both are melted.
Combine chocolate mixture with marsala, sugar, almond meal and combined coffee and the water in large bowl; beat in egg yolks, one at a time.
Beat egg whites in small bowl with electric mixer until soft peaks form; gently fold into chocolate mixture, in two batches. Pour mixture into prepared pan.
Bake in moderate oven about 45 minutes; cover with foil during baking if overbrowning. Cool cake in pan, cover; refrigerate several hours or overnight.
Carefully turn cake onto board; cut into slices with a hot knife. Dust cake with sifted icing sugar; serve with strawberry coulis and whipped cream, if desired.
Strawberry coulis Blend or process hulled strawberries and icing sugar until mixture is smooth.

serves 6

irish cream and dark chocolate mousse cake

We used Baileys Irish Cream in this recipe – a liqueur made of a blend of cream, Irish whiskey and Irish spirits.

6 eggs, separated
½ cup (80g) icing
    sugar mixture
¼ cup (25g) cocoa
    powder
2 tablespoons cornflour
150g dark eating
    chocolate, melted
1 tablespoon water
600ml thickened cream
450g dark eating
    chocolate, chopped
    coarsely, extra
¾ cup (180ml) irish
    cream liqueur
1 tablespoon cocoa
    powder, extra

Preheat oven to moderate. Grease 26cm x 32cm swiss roll pan; line base and sides with baking paper.

Beat egg yolks and sugar in small bowl with electric mixer until thick and creamy; transfer mixture to large bowl. Fold in combined sifted cocoa powder and cornflour, then chocolate; fold in the water.

Beat egg whites in medium bowl with electric mixer until soft peaks form. Fold egg whites, in two batches, into chocolate mixture. Spread mixture into prepared pan.

Bake in moderate oven about 15 minutes. Turn cake onto baking-paper-covered wire rack. Cover cake with baking paper; cool to room temperature.

Grease 22cm springform tin; line side with baking paper, bringing paper 5cm above edge of tin. Cut 22cm-diameter circle from cooled cake; place in prepared tin. Discard remaining cake.

Combine cream and extra chocolate in medium saucepan; stir over low heat until smooth. Transfer to large bowl; refrigerate until just cold.

Add liqueur to chocolate mixture; beat with electric mixer until mixture changes to a paler colour. Pour mixture into prepared tin; refrigerate about 3 hours or until set.

Transfer cake from tin to serving plate; dust with sifted extra cocoa powder.

serves 12
tip Do not overbeat the chocolate and liqueur mixture as it will curdle.

sticky chocolate date pudding

1⅓ cups (200g) seeded dried dates, chopped
1¾ cups (430ml) water
1 teaspoon bicarbonate of soda
80g butter, chopped
⅔ cup (150g) caster sugar
2 eggs
1 cup (150g) self-raising flour
⅓ cup (35g) cocoa powder
⅔ cup (70g) pecans, toasted, chopped
butterscotch sauce
1¼ cups (280g) firmly packed brown sugar
80g butter
300ml thickened cream

Preheat oven to moderate. Grease deep 22cm-round cake pan; line base with baking paper.
Combine dates and the water in small saucepan; bring to a boil. Remove from heat, add soda; cover, stand 5 minutes. Blend or process until smooth.
Beat butter and sugar in small bowl with electric mixer until combined; beat in eggs quickly, one at a time (mixture will curdle at this stage). Transfer mixture to large bowl; fold in sifted flour and cocoa powder, then add nuts and warm date mixture, in two batches. Pour mixture into prepared pan.
Bake in moderate oven about 1 hour. Stand pudding in pan 10 minutes, before turning onto serving plate.
Serve pudding with hot butterscotch sauce and whipped cream, if desired.
Butterscotch sauce Combine ingredients in medium saucepan; stir over heat, without boiling, until sugar is dissolved. Simmer, without stirring, 3 minutes.

serves 8 to 10

chocolate butterscotch cake

¼ cup (25g) cocoa powder
250g butter, chopped
1 cup (220g) firmly packed
   dark brown sugar
2 eggs
1 tablespoon golden syrup
1¼ cups (185g)
   self-raising flour
½ cup (125ml) milk
mascarpone cream
1 cup (250g)
   mascarpone cheese
300ml thickened cream
caramel icing
60g butter
½ cup (110g) firmly packed
   dark brown sugar
¼ cup (60ml) milk
1½ cups (240g) icing
   sugar mixture

Preheat oven to moderate. Grease deep 20cm-round cake pan; line base and side with baking paper.

Sift cocoa powder into large bowl; add remaining ingredients. Beat with electric mixer on low speed until combined. Increase speed to medium; beat until mixture has just changed in colour. Pour mixture into prepared pan.

Bake in moderate oven about 1 hour. Stand cake in pan 10 minutes, then turn, top-side up, onto wire rack to cool.

Using large serrated knife, split cake into three layers. Place one layer on serving plate; spread with a third of the mascarpone cream and a third of the caramel icing. Repeat with second layer and half of the remaining mascarpone cream and half of the remaining caramel icing; top with remaining cake layer. Cover top cake layer with remaining mascarpone cream then drizzle with remaining caramel icing. Swirl for marbled effect; refrigerate about 30 minutes or until icing is firm.

Mascarpone cream Whisk mascarpone and cream in small bowl until soft peaks form.

Caramel icing Heat butter, brown sugar and milk in small saucepan, stirring constantly, without boiling, until sugar dissolves; remove from heat. Add icing sugar; stir until smooth.

serves 10

tip Do not overbeat the mascarpone cream mixture as it could curdle.

gluten-free chocolate cake

You need 1 large overripe banana (230g) for this recipe.

1 cup (125g) soy flour
¾ cup (110g) corn cornflour
1¼ teaspoons bicarbonate of soda
½ cup (50g) cocoa powder
1¼ cups (275g) caster sugar
150g butter, melted
1 tablespoon white vinegar
1 cup (250ml) evaporated milk
2 eggs
½ cup mashed banana
2 tablespoons raspberry jam
300ml thickened cream, whipped

Preheat oven to moderate. Grease two 22cm-round sandwich pans; line bases with baking paper.
Sift flours, soda, cocoa powder and sugar into large bowl; add butter, vinegar and milk. Beat with electric mixer on low speed 1 minute; add eggs, banana and jam, beat on medium speed 2 minutes. Pour cake mixture into prepared pans.
Bake in moderate oven about 30 minutes. Stand cakes in pans 5 minutes, before turning onto wire racks to cool.
Sandwich cakes with whipped cream.

serves 6 to 8

chocolate brownies with warm chocolate sauce

150g butter, chopped
300g dark eating chocolate, chopped coarsely
1½ cups (330g) firmly packed brown sugar
4 eggs, beaten lightly
1 cup (150g) plain flour
½ cup (120g) sour cream
½ cup (60g) hazelnuts, toasted, chopped coarsely
ice-cream for serving
warm chocolate sauce
150g dark eating chocolate, chopped coarsely
1 cup (250ml) cream
⅓ cup (75g) firmly packed brown sugar
2 teaspoons Frangelico or Tia Maria

Preheat oven to moderate. Line base and sides of 20cm x 30cm lamington pan with baking paper.
Combine butter and chocolate in medium saucepan; stir over low heat until chocolate is just melted. Transfer chocolate mixture to medium bowl; add sugar and egg to chocolate mixture, then sifted flour, sour cream and nuts. Spread mixture into prepared pan.
Bake in moderate oven about 30 minutes; cool in pan.
Cut warm brownie into 16 pieces. Serve brownies, topped with ice-cream and drizzled with warm chocolate sauce.
Warm chocolate sauce Combine chocolate, cream and sugar in small saucepan; stir over low heat until mixture is smooth. Simmer, uncovered, 1 minute. Remove from heat; stir in liqueur.

serves 8

tip The brownie and the sauce can be made up to two days ahead; store sauce, covered in the refrigerator. Reheat brownie and sauce gently before serving.

mississippi mud cake

This popular cake is a delectable alternative to fruit cake for weddings and other occasions. It is also wonderful after dinner with coffee, served warm or at room temperature with double cream.

250g butter, chopped
150g dark eating
   chocolate, chopped
2 cups (440g) caster sugar
1 cup (250ml) hot water
⅓ cup (80ml) coffee-
   flavoured liqueur
1 tablespoon instant
   coffee powder
1½ cups (225g) plain flour
¼ cup (35g)
   self-raising flour
¼ cup (25g) cocoa powder
2 eggs, beaten lightly

Preheat oven to moderately slow. Grease deep 20cm-round cake pan; line base and side with baking paper.

Combine butter, chocolate, sugar, the water, liqueur and coffee powder in medium saucepan. Using wooden spoon, stir over low heat until chocolate melts.

Transfer mixture to large bowl; cool 15 minutes. Whisk in combined sifted flours and cocoa powder, then egg. Pour mixture into prepared pan.

Bake in moderately slow oven about 1½ hours. Stand cake in pan 30 minutes, before turning onto wire rack; turn cake top-side up to cool.

serves 10

tips Any coffee or chocolate-flavoured liqueur (Tia Maria, Kahlua or Crème de Cacao) can be used in this recipe.

Cover the cake loosely with foil about halfway through the baking time if it starts to overbrown. This cake will keep for up to one week if kept in an airtight container in the refrigerator.

chocolate panforte

Rice paper is a fine, edible paper; contrary to popular belief, it is not actually made from rice, but from the pith of a small tree that grows in Asia. Rice paper can be found in specialist-food stores and some delicatessens.

2 sheets rice paper
¾ cup (110g) plain flour
2 tablespoons cocoa powder
½ teaspoon ground cinnamon
½ teaspoon ground ginger
½ cup (150g) coarsely chopped
   glacé figs
½ cup (85g) dried dates,
   seeded, halved
½ cup (125g) coarsely chopped
   glacé peaches
¼ cup (50g) red glacé cherries, halved
¼ cup (50g) green glacé
   cherries, halved
½ cup (80g) blanched almonds, toasted
½ cup (75g) unsalted cashews, toasted
½ cup (75g) hazelnuts, toasted
½ cup (75g) macadamia nuts, toasted
¹/₃ cup (120g) honey
¹/₃ cup (75g) caster sugar
¹/₃ cup (75g) firmly packed brown sugar
2 tablespoons water
100g dark eating chocolate, melted

Preheat oven to moderately slow. Grease 20cm sandwich pan; line base with rice paper sheets.

Sift flour, cocoa powder and spices into large bowl; stir in fruit and nuts.

Combine honey, sugars and the water in small saucepan; stir over heat, without boiling, until sugar dissolves. Simmer; uncovered, without stirring, 5 minutes. Pour hot syrup then chocolate into nut mixture; stir until well combined. Press mixture firmly into prepared pan.

Bake in moderately slow oven about 45 minutes; cool in pan.

Remove panforte from pan; wrap in foil. Stand overnight; cut into thin wedges to serve.

serves 30

chocolate roulade with coffee cream

Tia Maria, Kahlua and Crème de Caçao are all coffee-flavoured liqueurs; any one of them can be used in this recipe.

1 tablespoon
   caster sugar
200g dark eating
   chocolate, chopped
   coarsely
¼ cup (60ml) hot water
1 tablespoon instant
   coffee powder
4 eggs, separated
½ cup (110g) caster
   sugar, extra
1 teaspoon hot
   water, extra
300ml thickened cream
2 tablespoons coffee-
   flavoured liqueur
1 tablespoon icing
   sugar mixture

Preheat oven to moderate. Grease 26cm x 32cm swiss roll pan; line base with baking paper.

Place a piece of baking paper cut the same size as swiss roll pan on board or bench; sprinkle evenly with caster sugar.

Combine chocolate, the water and half of the coffee powder in large heatproof bowl. Stir over large saucepan of simmering water until smooth; remove from heat.

Beat egg yolks and extra caster sugar in small bowl with electric mixer until thick and creamy; fold egg mixture into warm chocolate mixture.

Meanwhile, beat egg whites in small bowl with electric mixer until soft peaks form; fold egg whites, in two batches, into chocolate mixture. Spread into prepared pan.

Bake in moderate oven about 10 minutes. Turn cake onto sugared paper, peeling baking paper away; use serrated knife to cut away crisp edges from all sides. Cover cake with tea towel; cool.

Dissolve remaining coffee powder in the extra water in small bowl; cool. Add cream, liqueur and icing sugar; beat with electric mixer until firm peaks form. Spread cake evenly with cream mixture.

Roll cake, from long side, by lifting paper and using it to guide the roll into shape. Cover roll; refrigerate 30 minutes before serving.

serves 8

tip Be sure you beat the egg yolk mixture until thick, and the egg whites only until soft peaks form. Overbeating will dry out the egg whites and make them difficult to fold into the chocolate mixture.

upside-down chocolate caramel nut cake

2 tablespoons chopped, unsalted, roasted macadamias
2 tablespoons chopped, unsalted, roasted pistachios
2 tablespoons chopped, unsalted, roasted walnuts
125g butter, chopped
1 cup (220g) firmly packed brown sugar
3 eggs
1 cup (150g) self-raising flour
¼ cup (35g) plain flour
¼ teaspoon bicarbonate of soda
⅓ cup (35g) cocoa powder
100g dark eating chocolate, melted
¾ cup (180ml) milk
caramel topping
40g butter
¼ cup (55g) firmly packed brown sugar
2 tablespoons cream

Preheat oven to moderately slow. Grease deep 20cm-round cake pan; line base with baking paper.

Pour hot caramel topping over base of prepared pan, sprinkle combined nuts over caramel; freeze while preparing cake mixture.

Beat butter and sugar in small bowl with electric mixer until light and fluffy. Beat in eggs, one at a time, until just combined between each addition.

Stir in sifted flours, bicarbonate of soda and cocoa powder, then chocolate and milk. Spread cake mixture over caramel nut topping.

Bake in moderately slow oven about 1 hour and 10 minutes. Stand cake in pan 15 minutes, before turning onto wire rack to cool.

Caramel topping Combine butter, sugar and cream in small saucepan; stir over low heat, without boiling, until sugar is dissolved. Bring to a boil, then remove from heat.

serves 10

tip This cake can be made a day ahead and kept in an airtight container.

low-fat chocolate fudge cake

85g dark eating chocolate, chopped finely
½ cup (50g) cocoa powder
1 cup (200g) firmly packed brown sugar
½ cup (125ml) boiling water
2 egg yolks
¼ cup (30g) almond meal
⅓ cup (50g) wholemeal plain flour
4 egg whites

Preheat oven to moderate. Line base and side of
deep 20cm-round cake pan with baking paper.
Combine chocolate, cocoa and sugar with the water
in large bowl; stir until smooth. Add egg yolks; whisk
to combine. Fold in almond meal and flour.
Beat egg whites in small bowl with electric mixer until firm
peaks form. Gently fold egg white mixture into chocolate
mixture, in two batches; pour into prepared pan.
Bake in moderate oven about 40 minutes. Stand in pan
5 minutes. Turn onto wire rack; remove paper.

serves 8
tip Serve this cake warm, dusted with icing sugar and
topped with fresh strawberries.

microwave chocolate hazelnut cake

125g butter, chopped
1 cup (220g) caster sugar
1 cup (250ml) water
1 cup (150g) self-raising flour
1/3 cup (35g) cocoa powder
1/2 teaspoon bicarbonate of soda
1/2 cup (55g) hazelnut meal
2 eggs, beaten lightly
1 teaspoon vanilla essence
1/4 cup (35g) roasted hazelnuts, chopped coarsely
chocolate ganache
250g dark eating chocolate, chopped
3/4 cup (180ml) thickened cream

Grease 21cm microwave-safe ring pan. Line base
with baking paper.
Combine butter, sugar and the water in large microwave-safe
bowl; cook, uncovered on HIGH (100%) 4 minutes, stirring
once during cooking. Cool to room temperature.
Sift flour, cocoa powder and soda into butter mixture; add
hazelnut meal and whisk until mixture is smooth. Stir in
egg and essence. Pour mixture into prepared pan and
place on a microwave-safe rack in the oven.
Cook, uncovered, on MEDIUM-HIGH (70-80%) about
10 minutes or until almost cooked in the centre. Stand cake
in pan 5 minutes, before turning onto wire rack to cool.
Spread top and sides of cake with chocolate ganache
and sprinkle with hazelnuts.
Chocolate ganache Combine chocolate and cream
in small microwave-safe bowl; cook, uncovered, on
HIGH (100%) 1 1/2 minutes. Stir until chocolate melts and
mixture is smooth; refrigerate, stirring occasionally, until
of a spreadable consistency.

serves 8
tip This cake is best made on day of serving.

glossary

almonds flat, pointy-ended nuts with pitted brown shell enclosing a creamy white kernel that is covered by a brown skin.

blanched: brown skins removed.

flaked: paper-thin slices.

meal: also known as ground almonds; nuts are powdered to a coarse flour texture, for use in baking or as a thickening agent.

bicarbonate of soda also known as baking soda.

butter use salted or unsalted (sweet) butter; 125g is equal to one stick of butter.

buttermilk sold in refrigerated dairy compartments in most supermarkets. Originally just the liquid left after cream was separated from milk, today it is commercially made similarly to yogurt.

cashews we used unsalted, roasted cashews.

chocolate

dark eating: made of cocoa liquor, cocoa butter and sugar.

milk cooking: we used cooking-quality chocolate.

white cooking: we used cooking-quality chocolate.

cocoa powder also known as cocoa; unsweetened, dried, roasted and ground cocoa beans.

coffee-flavoured liqueur Tia Maria, Kahlua or any generic brand.

cointreau colourless, orange-flavoured liqueur.

cornflour also known as cornstarch; used as a thickening agent in cooking. Available as wheaten cornflour and 100% corn cornflour (which is gluten free).

cream

sour: (minimum fat content 35%) a thick, commercially-cultured soured cream.

thick: we used thick cream with 48% fat content.

thickened: (minimum fat content 35%) a whipping cream containing a thickener.

crème de cacao chocolate-flavoured liqueur.

currants dried, tiny, almost black raisins so-named after a grape variety that originated in Corinth, Greece.

dark rum we prefer to use an underproof rum (not overproof) for a more subtle flavour.

dates, dried from the date palm tree; has a sticky texture, sometimes sold already pitted and chopped.

essence also known as extract; generally the by-product of distillation of plants. Can be set in alcohol or in a more pure form in glycerine.

evaporated milk unsweetened, canned milk from which water has been extracted by evaporation.

flour

plain: an all-purpose flour, made from wheat.

self-raising: plain flour sifted with baking powder in the proportion of 1 cup flour to 2 teaspoons baking powder.

soy: flour made from ground soy beans.

wholemeal plain: also known as all-purpose wholemeal flour.

frangelico hazelnut-flavoured liqueur.

gelatine we used powdered gelatine; also available in sheet form known as leaf gelatine.

glacé fruit also known as candied fruit. Fruit is cooked in heavy sugar syrup then dried.

golden syrup a by-product of refined sugarcane; pure maple syrup or honey can be substituted.

hazelnuts also known as filberts; plump, grape-size, rich, sweet nut having a brown inedible skin that is removed by rubbing heated nuts together vigorously in a tea towel.

meal: also known as ground hazelnuts; roasted nuts are powdered to a flour-like texture for use in baking.

honey the variety sold in a squeezable container is not suitable for the recipes in this book.

jam also known as preserve or conserve.

kahlua coffee-flavoured liqueur.

kirsch cherry-flavoured liqueur.

macadamia native to Australia, a rich and buttery nut; store in refrigerator because of high oil content.

marsala a sweet fortified wine originally from Sicily.

mascarpone fresh, unripened, thick, triple-cream cheese with a delicately sweet, slightly acidic flavour.

mixed peel also known as candied citrus peel.

mixed spice blend of ground cinnamon, allspice, clove, coriander, mace and nutmeg.

pecans nut that is native to the United States; golden-brown, buttery and rich.

pistachios pale-green, delicately flavoured nut inside hard, off-white shells.

raisins dried sweet grapes.

rice paper contrary to popular belief, rice paper isn't made from rice, but from the pith of a small tree that grows in Asia. The fine, glossy paper is edible. This variety, which is generally imported from Holland, looks like a grainy sheet of white paper. It is used in confectionery-making and baking.

sugar we used coarse, granulated table sugar, unless otherwise specified.

brown: a soft, fine granulated sugar retaining molasses for its characteristic colour and flavour.

caster: also known as superfine or finely granulated table sugar.

icing sugar mixture: also known as confectioners' sugar or powdered sugar; pulverised, granulated sugar crushed together with a small amount (about 3%) cornflour added.

sultanas also known as golden raisins; dried, seedless white grapes.

tia maria coffee-flavoured liqueur.

walnuts rich, crisp-textured nuts with crinkled surfaces and an astringent flavour.

vinegar, white made from spirit of cane sugar.

index

facts & figures

These conversions are approximate only, but the difference between an exact and the approximate conversion of various liquid and dry measures is minimal and will not affect your cooking results.

Measuring equipment
The difference between one country's measuring cups and another's is, at most, within a 2 or 3 teaspoon variance. (For the record, 1 Australian metric measuring cup holds approximately 250ml.) The most accurate way of measuring dry ingredients is to weigh them. For liquids, use a clear glass or plastic jug having metric markings.

Note: NZ, Canada, US and UK all use 15ml tablespoons. Australian tablespoons measure 20ml. All cup and spoon measurements are level.

How to measure
When using graduated measuring cups, shake dry ingredients loosely into the appropriate cup. Do not tap the cup on a bench or tightly pack the ingredients unless directed to do so. Level the top of measuring cups and measuring spoons with a knife. When measuring liquids, place a clear glass or plastic jug having metric markings on a flat surface to check accuracy at eye level.

Dry measures

metric	imperial
15g	½oz
30g	1oz
60g	2oz
90g	3oz
125g	4oz (¼lb)
155g	5oz
185g	6oz
220g	7oz
250g	8oz (½lb)
280g	9oz
315g	10oz
345g	11oz
375g	12oz (¾lb)
410g	13oz
440g	14oz
470g	15oz
500g	16oz (1lb)
750g	24oz (1½lb)
1kg	32oz (2lb)

We use large eggs with an average weight of 60g.

Liquid measures

metric	imperial
30 ml	1 fluid oz
60 ml	2 fluid oz
100 ml	3 fluid oz
125 ml	4 fluid oz
150 ml	5 fluid oz (¼ pint/1 gill)
190 ml	6 fluid oz
250 ml (1cup)	8 fluid oz
300 ml	10 fluid oz (½ pint)
500 ml	16 fluid oz
600 ml	20 fluid oz (1 pint)
1000 ml (1litre)	1¾ pints

Helpful measures

metric	imperial
3mm	⅛in
6mm	¼in
1cm	½in
2cm	¾in
2.5cm	1in
6cm	2½in
8cm	3in
20cm	8in
23cm	9in
25cm	10in
30cm	12in (1ft)

Oven temperatures
These oven temperatures are only a guide. Always check the manufacturer's manual.

	°C (Celsius)	°F (Fahrenheit)	Gas Mark
Very slow	120	250	½
Slow	140 – 150	275 – 300	1 – 2
Moderately slow	170	325	3
Moderate	180 – 190	350 – 375	4 – 5
Moderately hot	200	400	6
Hot	220 – 230	425 – 450	7 – 8
Very hot	240	475	9

at your fingertips

These elegant slipcovers store up to 10 mini books and make the books instantly accessible.

And the metric measuring cups and spoons make following our recipes a piece of cake.

Book Holder
Australia and overseas:
$8.95 (incl. GST).

Metric Measuring Set
Australia: $6.50 (incl. GST).
New Zealand: $A8.00.
Elsewhere: $A9.95.
Prices include postage and handling. This offer is available in all countries.

Mail or fax Photocopy and complete the coupon below and post to ACP Books Reader Offer, ACP Publishing, GPO Box 4967, Sydney NSW 2001, or fax to (02) 9267 4967.

Phone Have your credit card details ready, then phone 136 116 (Mon-Fri, 8.00am-6.00pm; Sat, 8.00am-6.00pm).

Australian residents We accept the credit cards listed on the coupon, money orders and cheques.

Overseas residents We accept the credit cards listed on the coupon, drafts in $A drawn on an Australian bank, and also UK, NZ and US cheques in the currency of the country of issue. Credit card charges are at the exchange rate current at the time of payment.

Photocopy and complete coupon below

- -

☐ **Book Holder**   ☐ **Metric Measuring Set**
Please indicate number(s) required.

Mr/Mrs/Ms _____

Address _____

_____

Postcode _____ Country _____

Ph: Business hours ( ) _____

I enclose my cheque/money order for $ _____ payable to ACP Publishing.

OR: please charge $ _____ to my ☐ Bankcard ☐ Mastercard

☐ Visa ☐ American Express ☐ Diners Club

Expiry date ____ /____

| | | | | | | | | | | | | | | | |

Card number

Cardholder's signature _____

Please allow up to 30 days delivery within Australia.
Allow up to 6 weeks for overseas deliveries.
Both offers expire 31/12/05. HLMCC05

Food director Pamela Clark
Food editor Louise Patniotis
ACP BOOKS
Editorial director Susan Tomnay
Creative director Hieu Chi Nguyen
Senior editor Julie Collard
Designer Mary Keep
Sales director Brian Cearnes
Publishing manager (rights & new projects) Jane Hazell
Brand manager Renée Crea
Sales & marketing coordinator Gabrielle Botto
Pre-press Harry Palmer
Production manager Carol Currie
Chief executive officer John Alexander
Group publisher Pat Ingram
Publisher Sue Wannan
Editor-in-chief Deborah Thomas
Produced by ACP Books, Sydney.
Printing by Dai Nippon Printing in Korea.
Published by ACP Publishing Pty Limited, 54 Park St, Sydney;
GPO Box 4088, Sydney, NSW 2001.
Ph: (02) 9282 8618 Fax: (02) 9267 9438.
acpbooks@acp.com.au
www.acpbooks.com.au
To order books phone 136 116.
Send recipe enquiries to
Recipeenquiries@acp.com.au
Australia Distributed by Network Services, GPO Box 4088, Sydney, NSW 2001.
Ph: (02) 9282 8777 Fax: (02) 9264 3278.
United Kingdom Distributed by Australian Consolidated Press (UK), Moulton Park Business Centre, Red House Road, Moulton Park, Northampton, NN3 6AQ. Ph: (01604) 497 531 Fax: (01604) 497 533 acpukltd@aol.com
Canada Distributed by Whitecap Books Ltd, 351 Lynn Ave, North Vancouver, BC, V7J 2C4,
Ph: (604) 980 9852 Fax: (604) 980 8197
customerservice@whitecap.ca
www.whitecap.ca
New Zealand Distributed by Netlink Distribution Company, ACP Media Centre, Cnr Fanshawe and Beaumont Streets, Westhaven, Auckland; PO Box 47906, Ponsonby, Auckland, NZ.
Ph: (09) 366 9966 ask@ndcnz.co.nz
South Africa Distributed by PSD Promotions, 30 Diesel Road, Isando, Gauteng, Johannesburg; PO Box 1175, Isando, 1600, Gauteng, Johannesburg. Ph: (27 11) 392 6065/7 Fax: (27 11) 392 6079/80
orders@psdprom.co.za

Clark, Pamela.
The Australian Women's Weekly
Chocolate Cakes

Includes index.
ISBN 1 86396 362 6

1. Cake. 2. Cookery (Chocolate).
I. Title: Australian Women's Weekly.

641.8653

© ACP Publishing Pty Limited 2004
ABN 18 053 273 546

Cover Chocolate ganache and raspberry cake, page 24.
Stylist Julz Beresford
Photographer Brett Stevens
Home economists Nancy Duran, Susan Riggall
Back cover at left, Chocolate buttermilk cake, page 16; at right, Family chocolate cake, page 7.

First published 2004. Reprinted 2004, 2005.